Learn to Write Sight Words -
Shapes

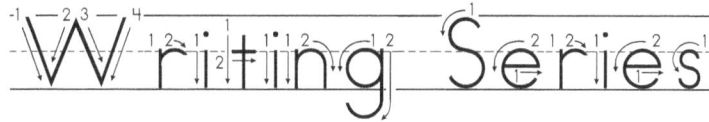

ISBN PAPERBACK: 978-1-956547-07-8

Names, characters, places, and incidents are the product of the author's imagination or are used fictitiously. Any resemblance to actual persons, living or dead, events, or locales is entirely coincidental.

Book design by Anne Lusher

Published by Unplanned Books, LLC.

UNPLANNED BOOKS

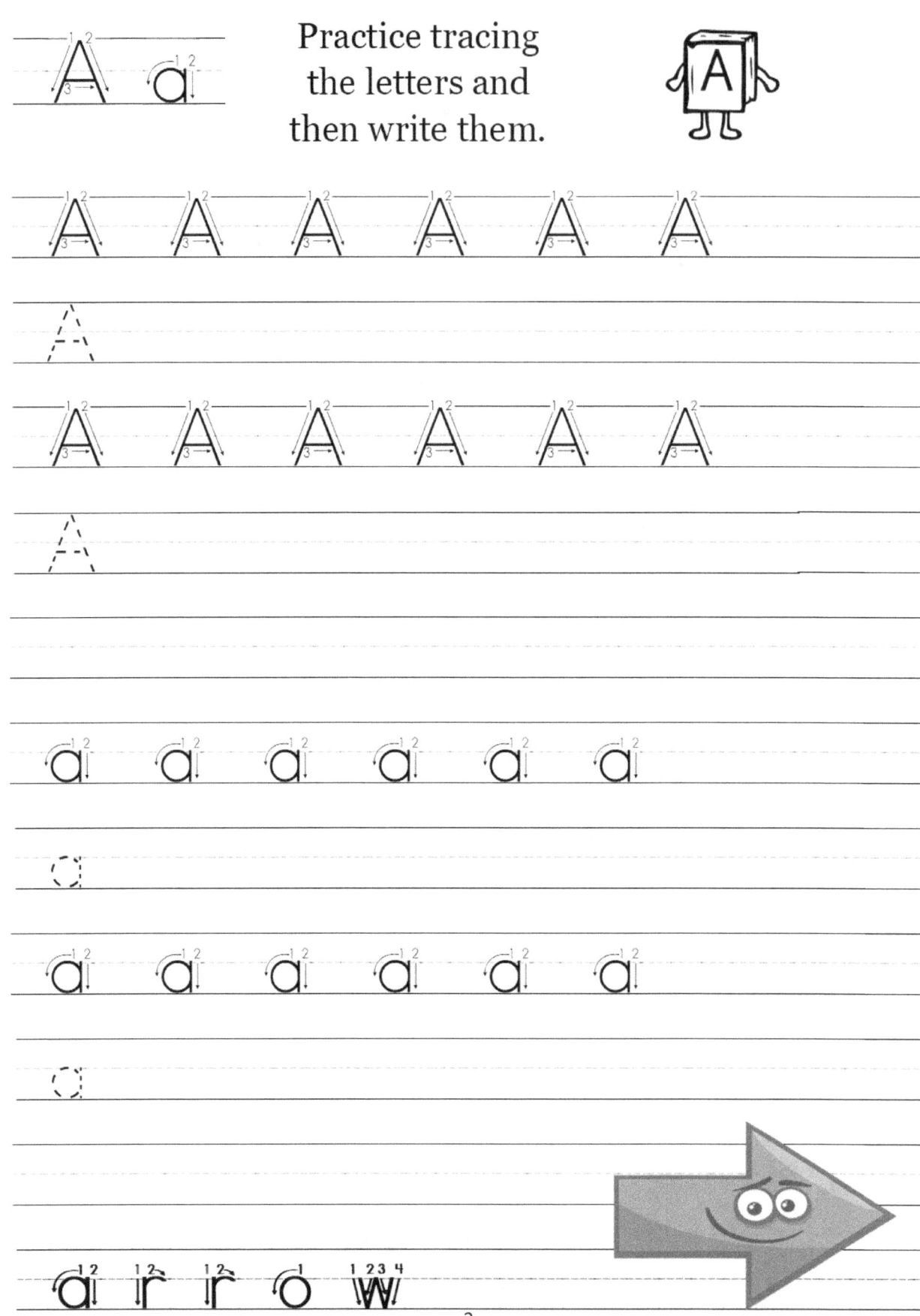

Practice tracing
the letters and
then write them.

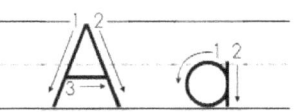 A a a

Trace and write the sight words.

add d d

add d

angle

angle

around

around

arrow

arrow

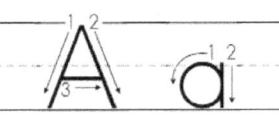 

Trace and write the
sight words, then read
aloud the definitions.

a d d

add: find the sum of

a n g l e

angle: space within lines

a r o u n d

around: in all directions

a r r o w

arrow: line with a pointy tip

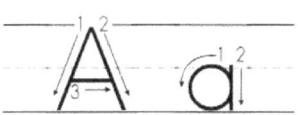 Use the examples
below to help write
new sentences.

Each triangle **angle** is equal.

I ran **around** with an **arrow**.

He can **add** the numbers.

B b

Practice tracing the letters and then write them.

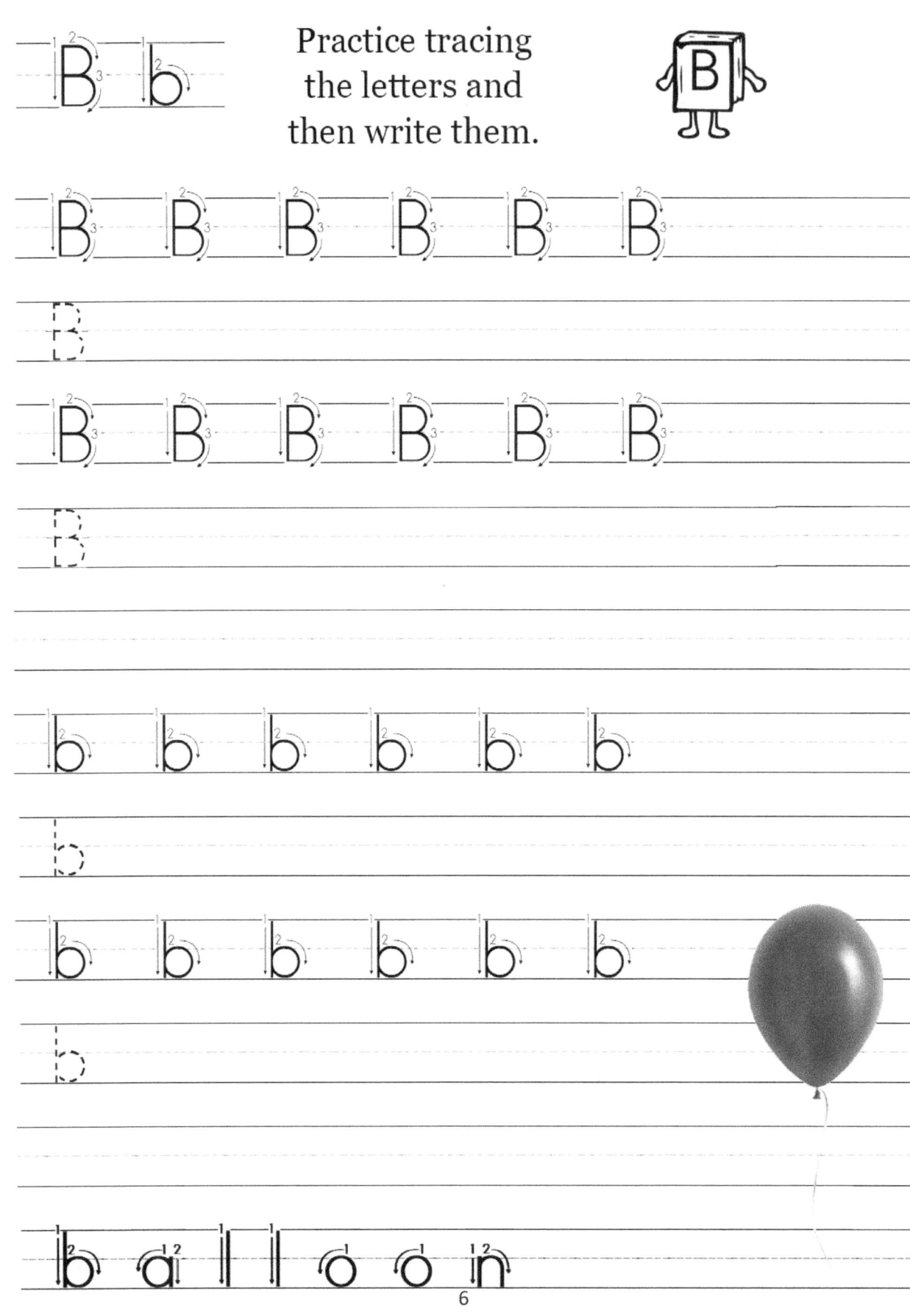

B B B B B B

B

B B B B B B

B

b b b b b b

b

b b b b b b

b

b a l l o o n

6

Trace and write the sight words.

before

before

below

below

both

both

balloon

balloon

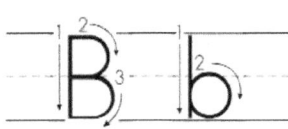

Trace and write the
sight words, then read
aloud the definitions.

before

before: in front of

below

below: underneath

both

both: one and the other

balloon

balloon: bag inflated with air

Use the examples
below to help write
new sentences.

Both boys went before me.

It was below the table.

I see a balloon.

BONUS WORDS FROM THE DANGER TWINS

The Danger Twins listed bonus sight words below. Write a sentence using any of the sight words.

answer   ball

age   been

are   best

C c

Practice tracing
the letters and
then write them.

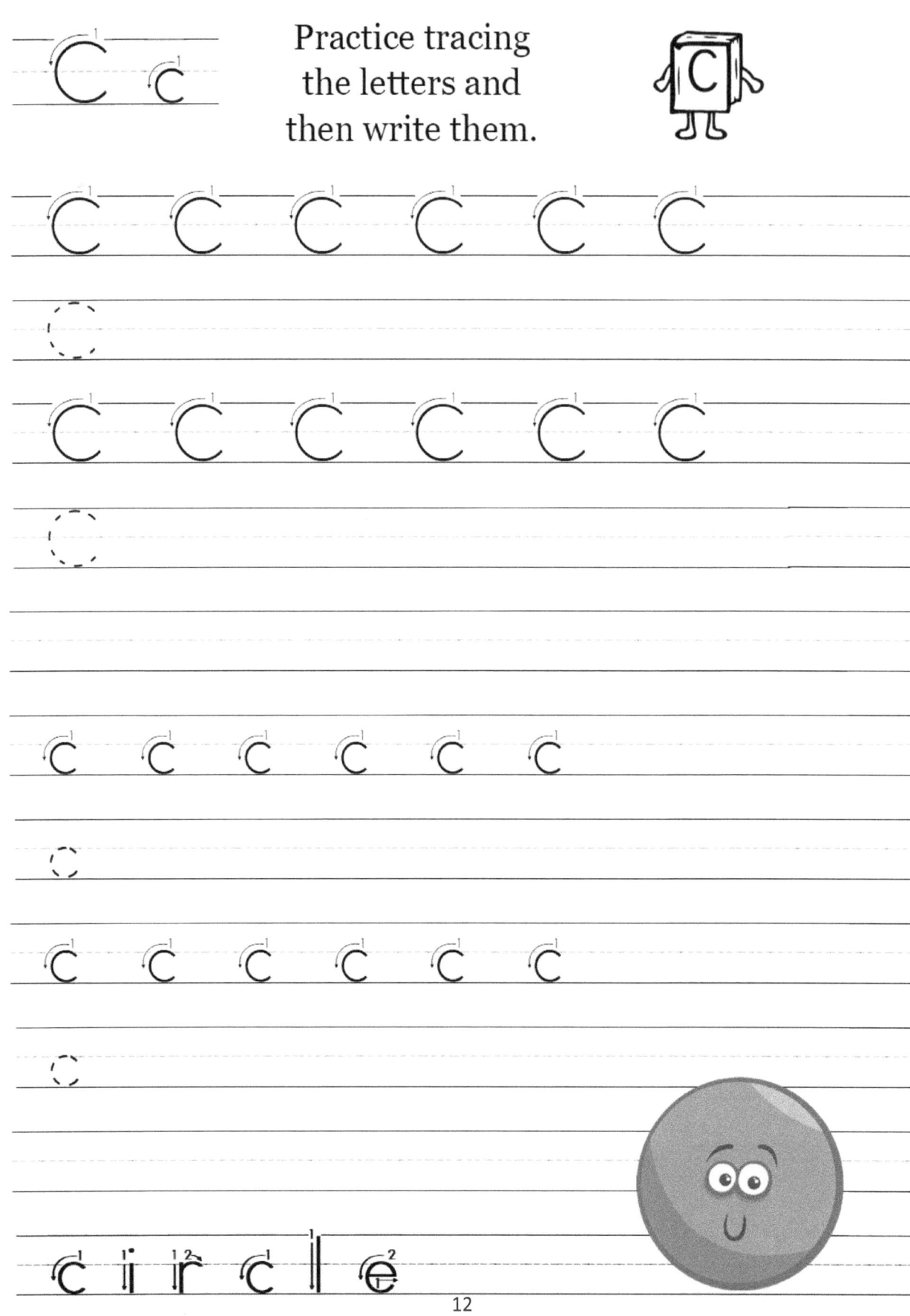

C C C C C C

C C C C C C

c c c c c c

c c c c c c

circle

12

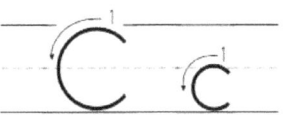

Trace and write the sight words.

center

center

common

common

count

count

circle

circle

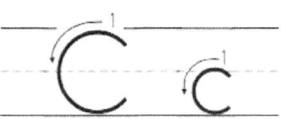 Trace and write the
sight words, then read
aloud the definitions.

c e n t e r

center: the middle point

c o m m o n

common: general, universal

c o u n t

count: to check over

c i r c l e

circle: line that loops around

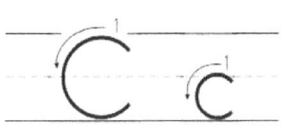

Use the examples
below to help write
new sentences.

We can **count** to 100.

That is **common** knowledge.

A **circle** has a **center** point.

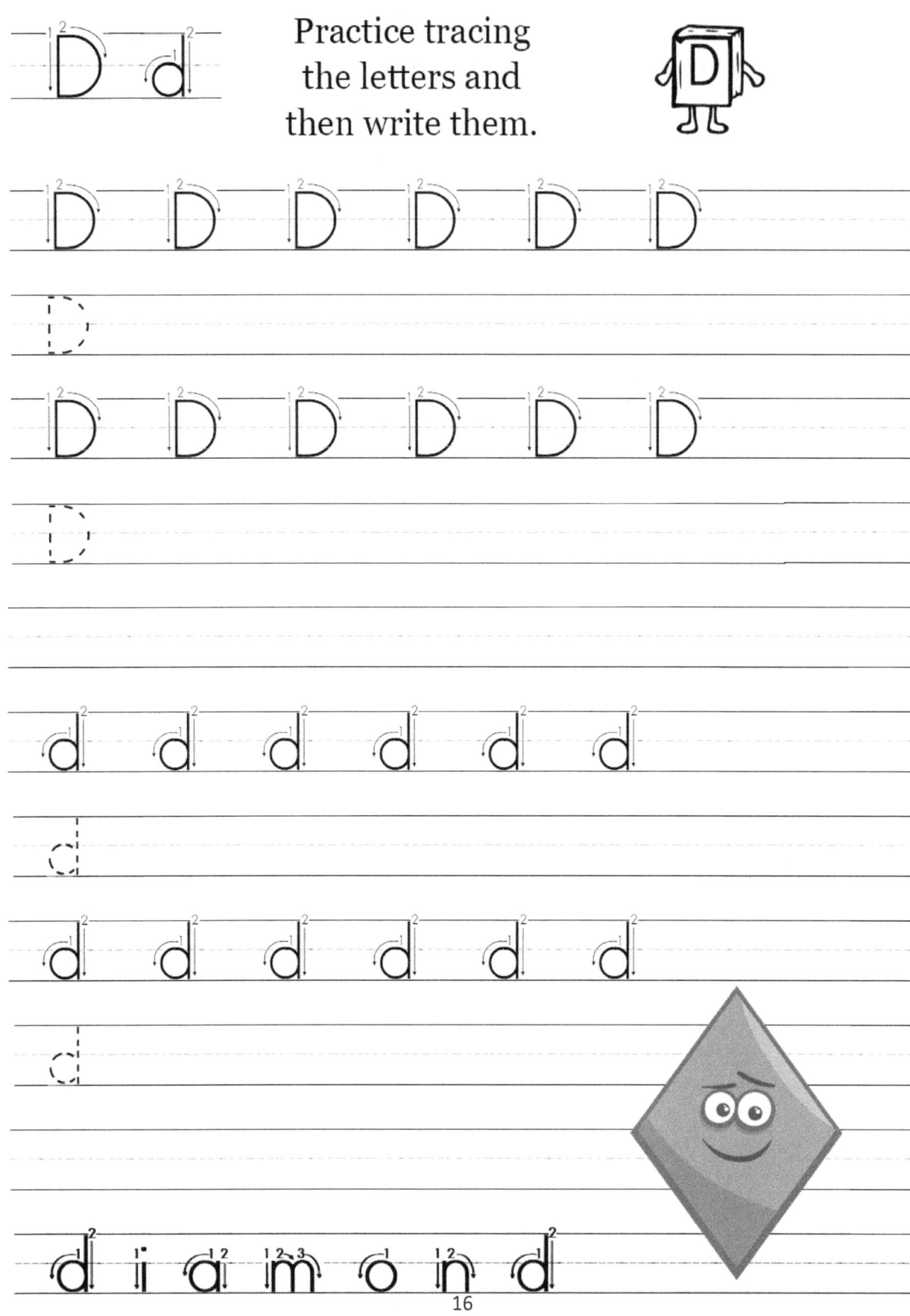

Practice tracing
the letters and
then write them.

diamond

16

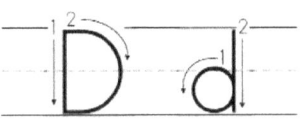

Trace and write
the sight words.

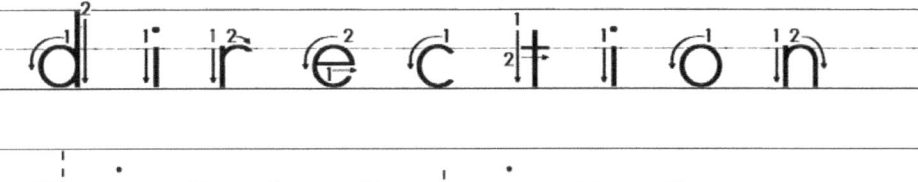

difference

direction

direction

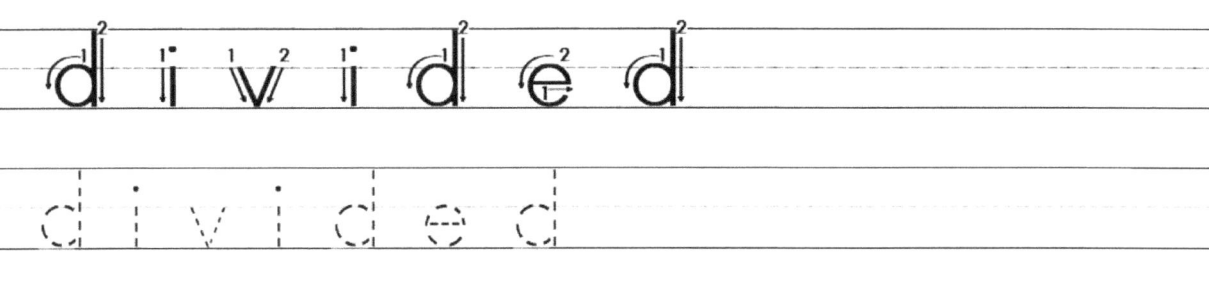

divided

diamond

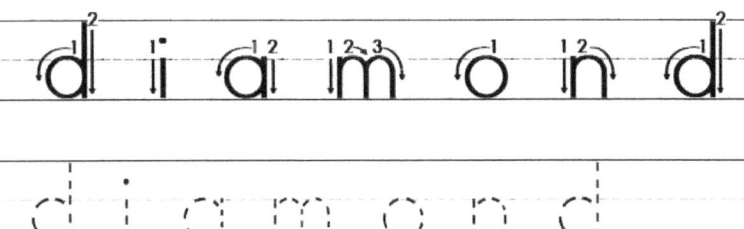

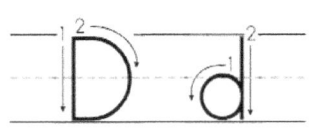 Trace and write the
sight words, then read
aloud the definitions.

difference

difference: dissimilar

direction

direction: path you take

divide

divide: to separate

diamond

diamond: rhombus-shaped

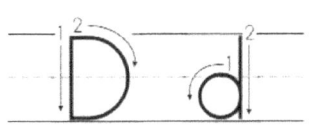 Use the examples below to help write new sentences.

The **difference** is ten.

North is a travel **direction**.

I cannot **divide** a **diamond**.

BONUS WORDS FROM THE DANGER TWINS

The Danger Twins listed bonus sight words below. Write a sentence using any of the sight words.

cloud distance

catch direct

correct down

Practice tracing the letters and then write them.

E e

E E E E E E

E

E E E E E E

E

e e e e e e

e

e e e e e e

e

ellipse

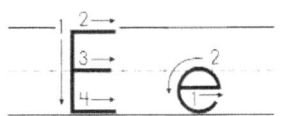 Trace and write
the sight words.

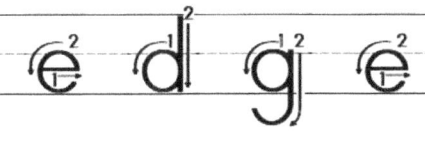

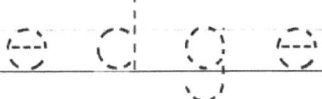

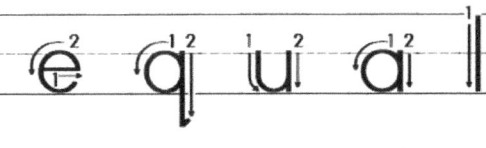

equal

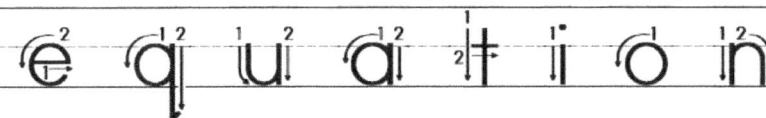

equation

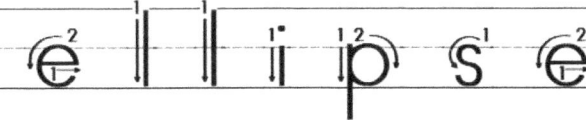

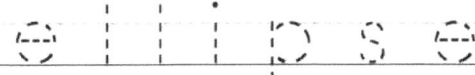

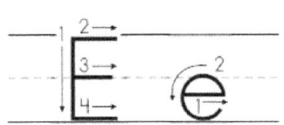 Trace and write the
sight words, then read
aloud the definitions.

edge

edge: where surface ends

equal

equal: alike in value

equation

equation: a math problem

ellipse

ellipse: similar to oval

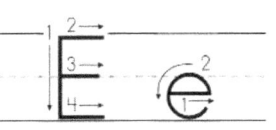

Use the examples
below to help write
new sentences.

Each edge is equal in size.

My equation was easy.

Eggs have an ellipse shape.

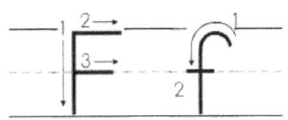 **Practice tracing the letters and then write them.**

F F F F F F

F

F F F F F F

F

f f f f f f

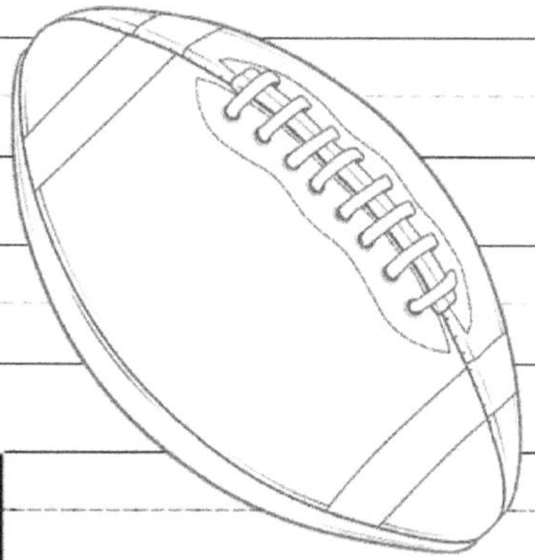

f

f f f f f f

f

f o o t b a l l

26

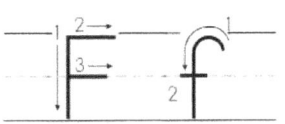

Trace and write the sight words.

feet

foot

few

figure

find

find

football

football

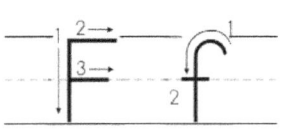

Trace and write the sight words, then read aloud the definitions.

feet

feet: plural of foot

few

few: not many

find

find: to locate attain

football

football: oval shape ball

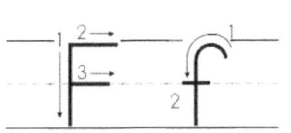

Use the examples
below to help write
new sentences.

We walked for a few feet.

I cannot **find** the answer.

He threw the football.

BONUS WORDS FROM THE DANGER TWINS

The Danger Twins listed bonus sight words below. Write a sentence using any of the sight words.

ears   foot

eight   four

even   first

G g

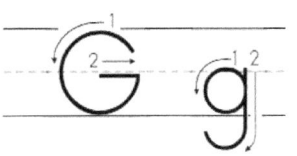

Practice tracing the letters and then write them.

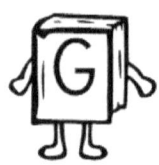

G G G G G G

G G G G G G

g g g g g g

g g g g g g

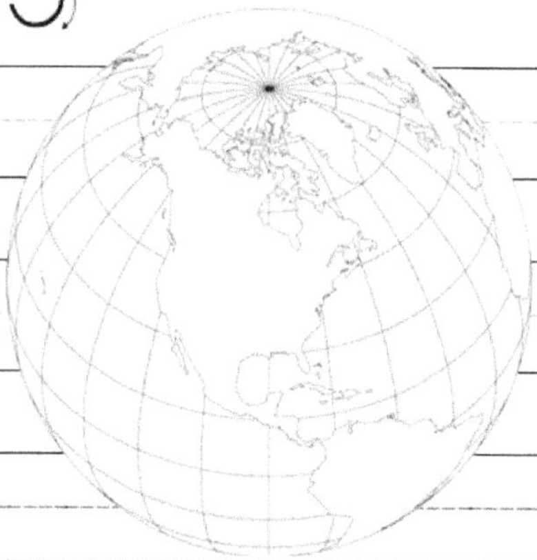

globe

Trace and write the sight words.

gave

gave

great

great

group

group

globe

globe

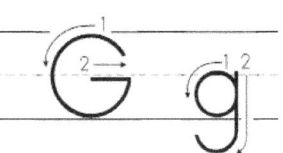 

Trace and write the
sight words, then read
aloud the definitions.

gave

gave: past tense of give

great

great: power; intensity

group

group: a number of things

globe

globe: a spherical shape

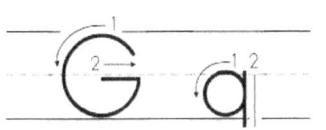

Use the examples
below to help write
new sentences.

The boy **gave** a gift.

It was a **great** surprise.

Our **group** liked the **globe**.

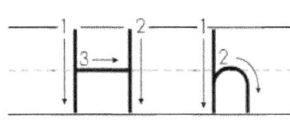

Practice tracing the letters and then write them.

H H H H H H

H

H H H H H H

H

h h h h h h

h

h h h h h h

h

h e x a g o n

36

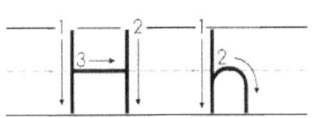

Trace and write
the sight words.

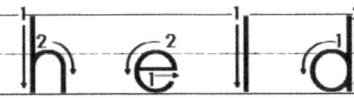

has

held

held

high

high

hexagon

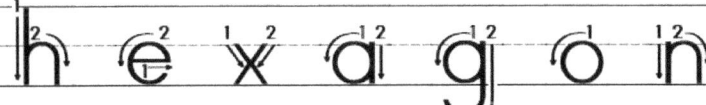

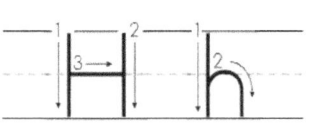 Trace and write the sight words, then read aloud the definitions.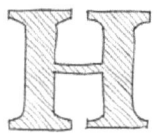

h a s

has: past tense of have

h e l d

held: past tense of to hold

h i g h

high: extend upward

h e x a g o n

hexagon: six sides

38

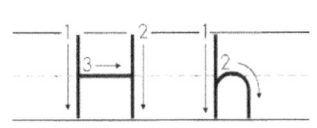

Use the examples
below to help write
new sentences.

He **has** one problem left.

I **held** it up **high**.

A stop sign is a **hexagon**.

BONUS WORDS FROM THE DANGER TWINS

The Danger Twins listed bonus sight words below. Write a sentence using any of the sight words.

good   have

game   hard

get   her

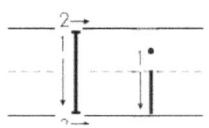

Practice tracing the letters and then write them.

I I I I I I I

I

I I I I I I I

I

i i i i i i i

i

i i i i i i i

i

i c e - c r e a m c o n e

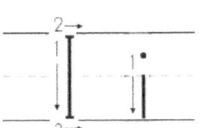

Trace and write
the sight words.

inches

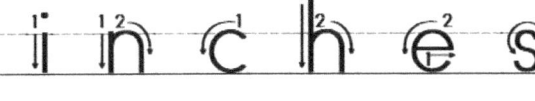

inches

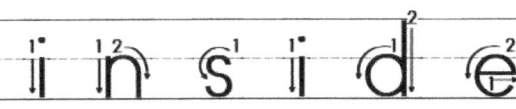

inside

inside

into

into

ice-cream cone

ice-cream cone

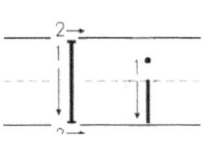

Trace and write the
sight words, then read
aloud the definitions.

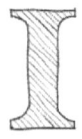

i n c h e s

inches: a unit of length

i n s i d e

inside: part of; within

i n t o

into: to the inside of

i c e - c r e a m   c o n e

ice-cream cone: conical shape

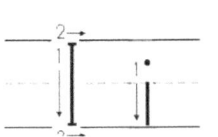

Use the examples
below to help write
new sentences.

The boy ran into a puddle.

The bug inside is 2 inches.

A see an ice-cream cone.

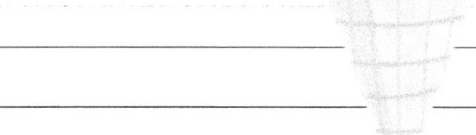

J j

Practice tracing
the letters and
then write them.

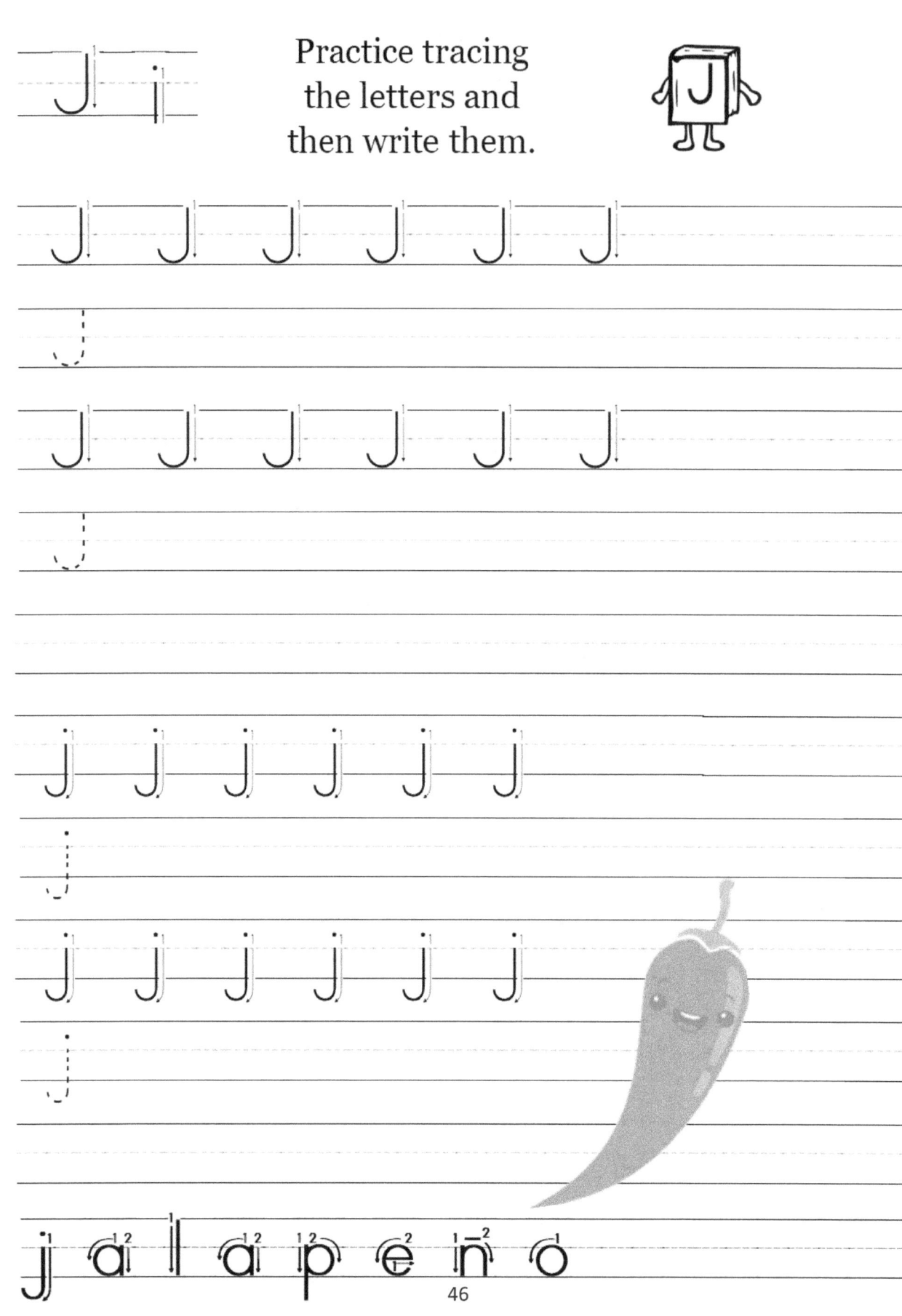

J J J J J J

J

J J J J J

J

j j j j j j

j

j j j j j j

j

jalapeño

46

Trace and write the sight words.

job

job

join

join

jumped

jumped

jalapeño

jalapeño

J j

Trace and write the sight words, then read aloud the definitions.

J

j o b

job: a piece of work

j o i n

join: to bring in contact

j u m p e d

jumped: rise suddenly

j a l a p e ñ o

jalapeño: a pointy pepper

 Use the examples
below to help write
new sentences.

Please join the group.

I jumped at the job offer.

He likes the jalapeño.

BONUS WORDS FROM THE DANGER TWINS

The Danger Twins listed bonus sight words below. Write a sentence using any of the sight words.

ice   jungle

include joke

into   juice

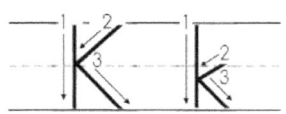

Practice tracing the letters and then write them.

K K K K K K

K

K K K K K K

K

k k k k k k

k

k k k k k k

k

kite

52

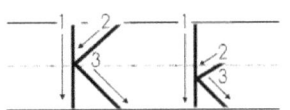

Trace and write the sight words.

kept
kept

king
king

know
know

kite
kite

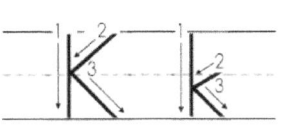

Trace and write the
sight words, then read
aloud the definitions.

kept

kept: to hold or retain

king

king: sovereign or monarch

know

know: to understand

kite

kite: has four sides

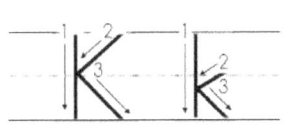 

Use the examples
below to help write
new sentences.

We kept the gift a secret.

The king rules the country.

I know she has the kite.

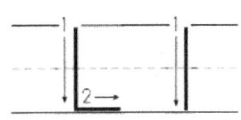

Practice tracing the letters and then write them.

L L L L L L

l

L L L L L L

l

I I I I I

I

I I I I I

I

lollipop

56

L l

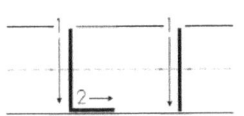

Trace and write the sight words.

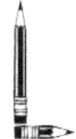

learn

learn

line

line

low

low

lollipop

lollipop

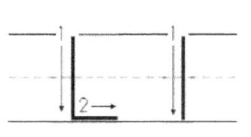

Trace and write the sight words, then read aloud the definitions.

learn

learn: to acquire knowledge

list

list: One item after another

low

low: not high or tall

lollipop

lollipop: ball of sugar

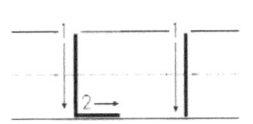

Use the examples
below to help write
new sentences.

I like to learn new things.

Add one lollipop to the list.

My book is on a low shelf.

BONUS WORDS FROM THE DANGER TWINS

The Danger Twins listed bonus sight words below. Write a sentence using any of the sight words.

kick   lake

key   leaf

knock   light

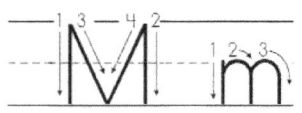 Practice tracing
the letters and
then write them.

M M M M M M

M

M M M M M M

M

m m m m m m

m

m m m m m m

m

moon

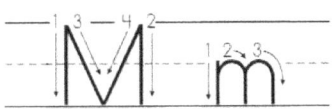

Trace and write
the sight words.

many

many

mile

mile

miss

miss

moon

moon

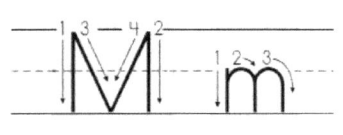 Trace and write the
sight words, then read
aloud the definitions.

many

many: a large number

mile

mile: unit of distance

miss

miss: fail to hit

moon

moon: the Earth's satellite

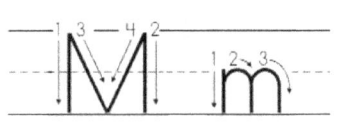 Use the examples
below to help write
new sentences.

He ran a mile many times.

I will not miss the target.

The moon has craters.

N n

Practice tracing
the letters and
then write them.

N N N N N N

N

N N N N N N

N

n n n n n n

n

n n n n n n

n

nonagon

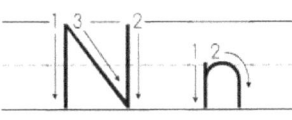

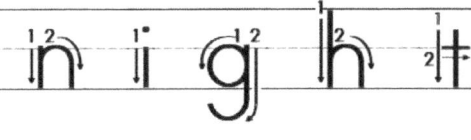

night

night

not

not

note

note

nonagon

nonagon

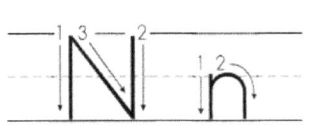

Trace and write the
sight words, then read
aloud the definitions.

night

night: sun setting

not

not: denial; refusal

note

note: a brief record

nonagon

nonagon: has nine sides

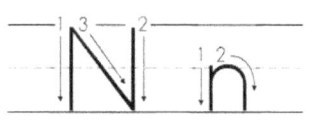

Use the examples
below to help write
new sentences.

I did **not** solve the problem.

We found a **note** last **night**

She can see the **nonagon**.

BONUS WORDS FROM THE DANGER TWINS

The Danger Twins listed bonus sight words below. Write a sentence using any of the sight words.

math   near

mix   north

map   never

Practice tracing
the letters and
then write them.

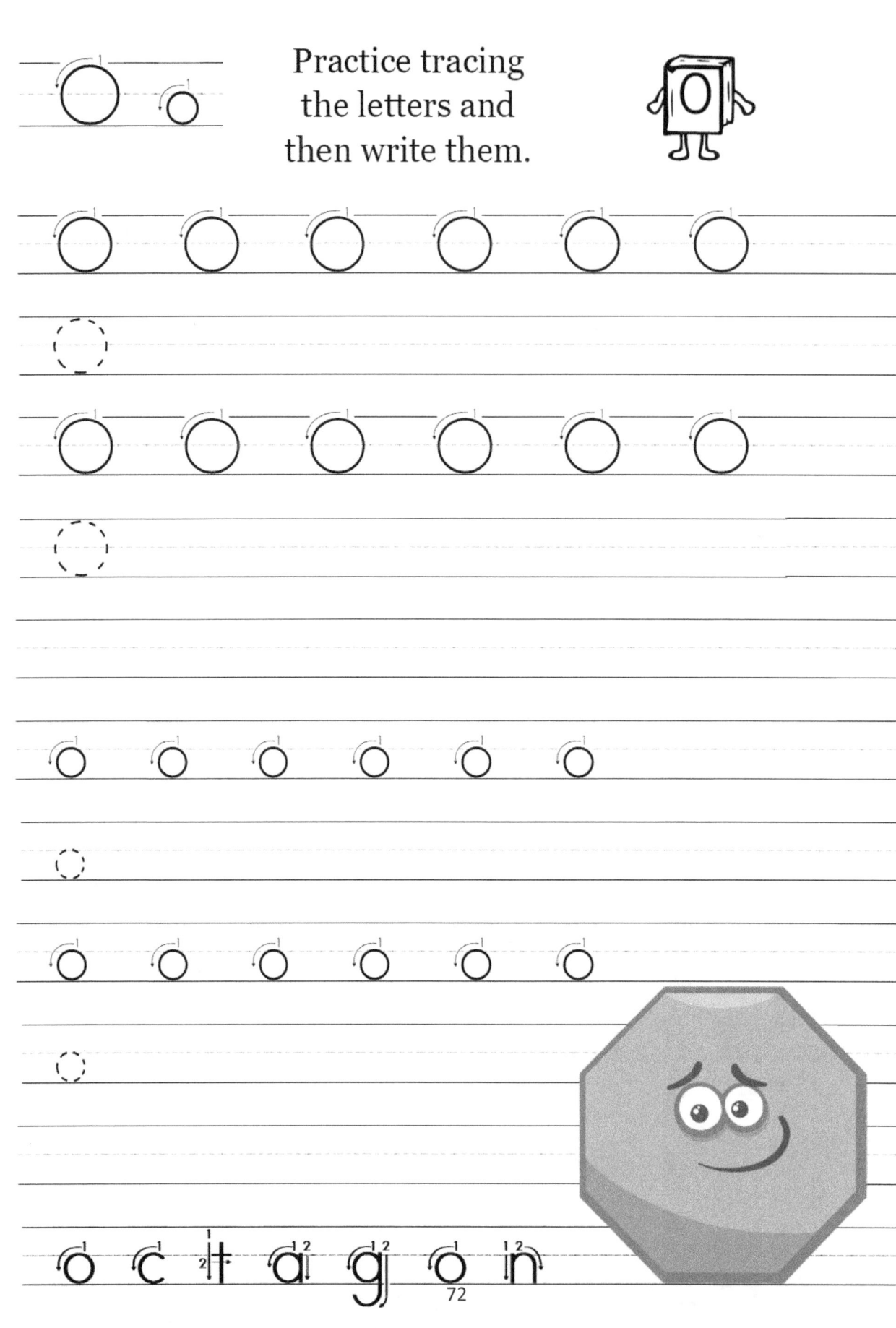

octagon

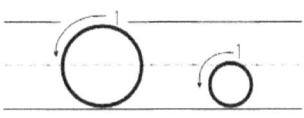

Trace and write
the sight words.

only

only

other

other

our

our

octagon

octagon

O o

Trace and write the sight words, then read aloud the definitions.

O

o n l y

only: without others

o t h e r

other: additional

o u r

our: possessive we

o c t a g o n

octagon: eight-sided

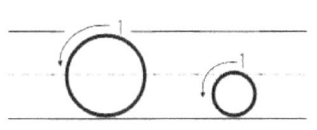

Use the examples
below to help write
new sentences.

Only our mom can help.

He would like the **other** one

The shape is an **octagon**.

P p Practice tracing
the letters and
then write them.

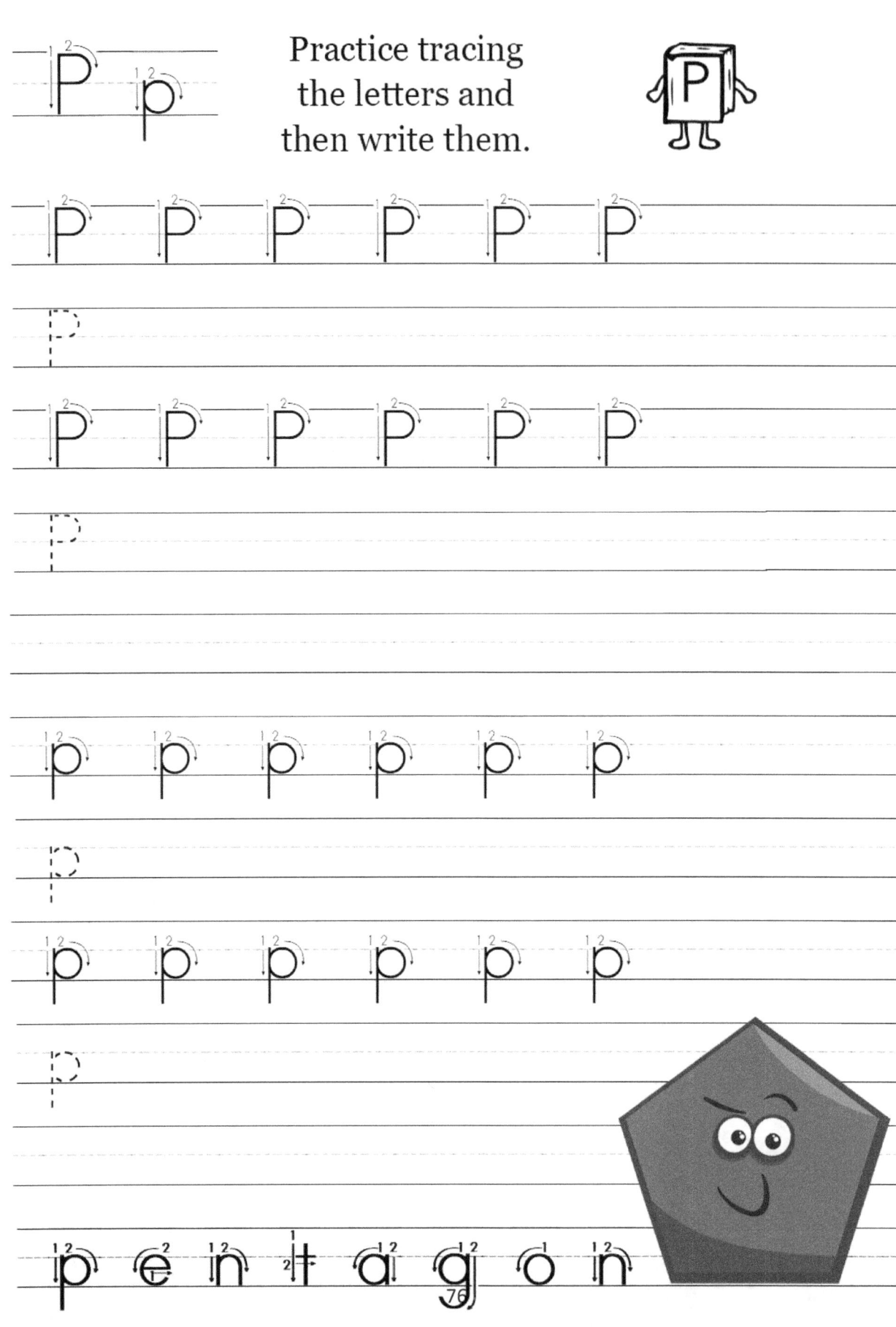

P P P P P P

P

P P P P P P

P

p p p p p p

p

p p p p p p

p

pentagon

76

Trace and write the sight words.

point

point

practice

practice

problem

problem

pentagon

pentagon

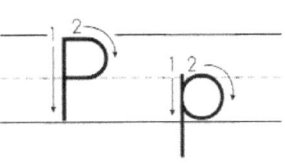 Trace and write the
sight words, then read
aloud the definitions.

point

point: guesture at someone

practice

practice: a habit; custom

problem

problem: it involves doubt

pentagon

pentagon: five sided

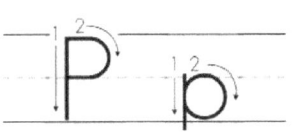 Use the examples below to help write new sentences.

I can **point** to the **problem**.

Practice solving the riddle.

We see a **pentagon** below.

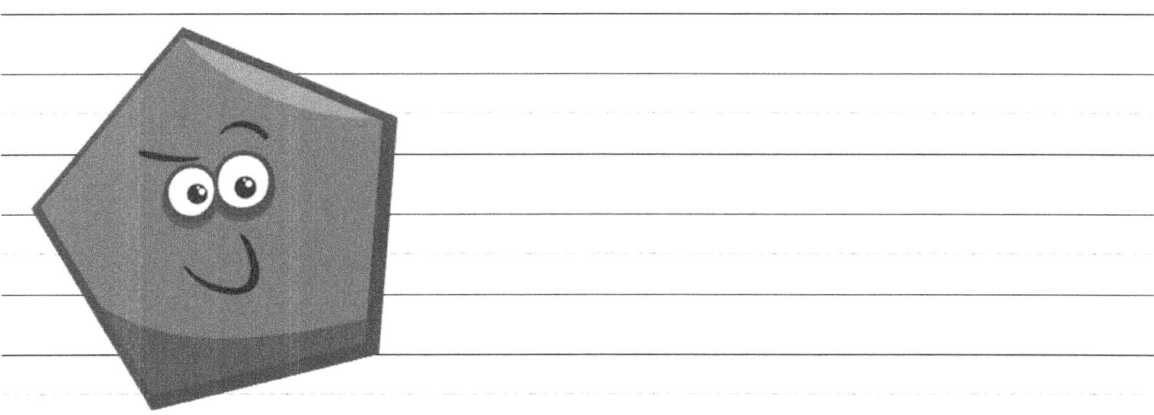

BONUS WORDS FROM THE DANGER TWINS

The Danger Twins listed bonus sight words below. Write a sentence using any of the sight words.

often   paint

once   pattern

order   penny

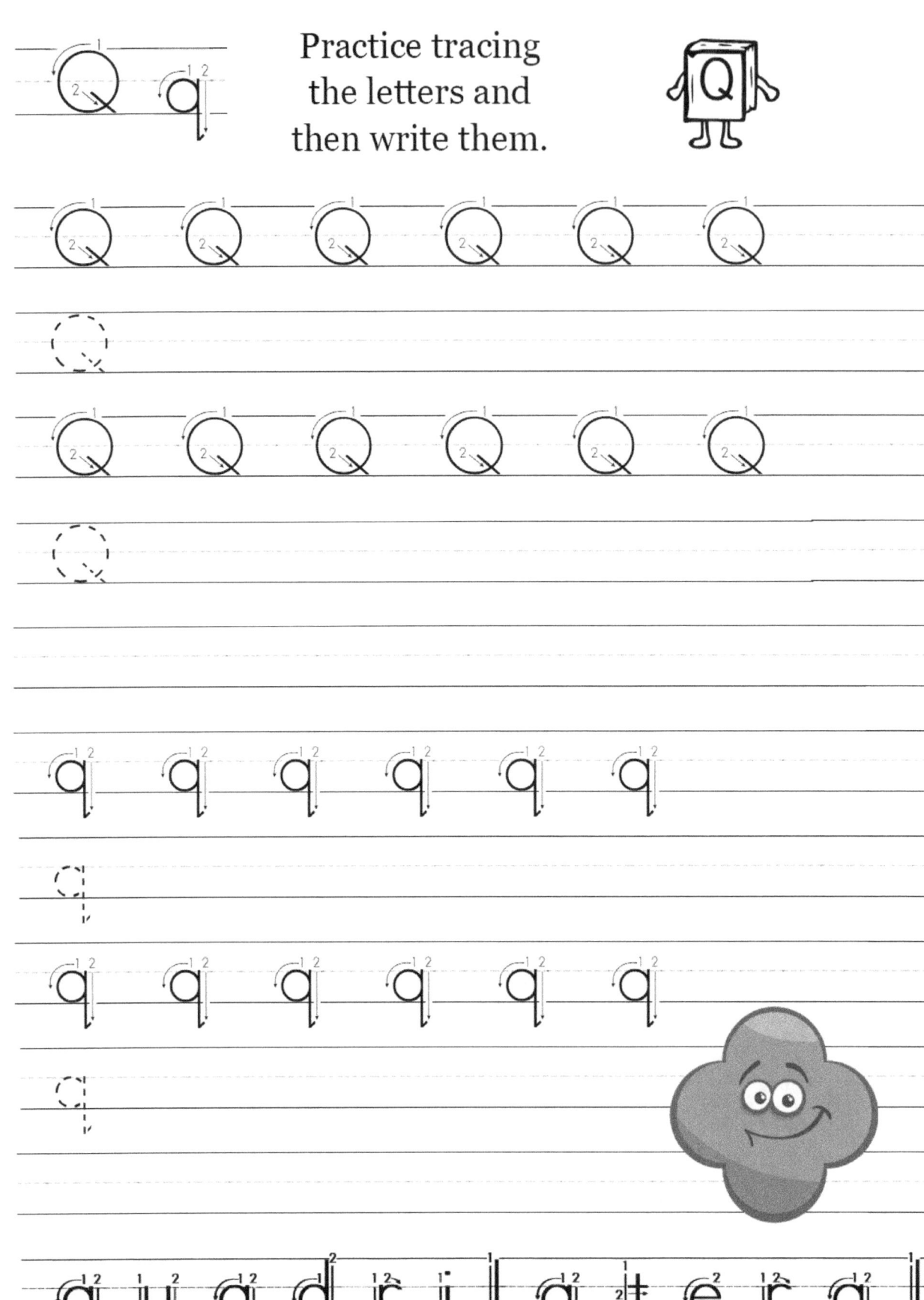

Practice tracing
the letters and
then write them.

quadrilateral

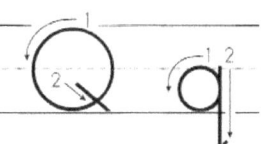

Trace and write
the sight words.

question

question

quickly

quickly

quite

quite

quadrilateral

quadrilateral

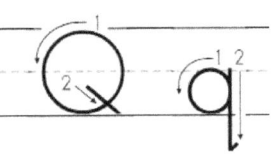

Trace and write the sight words, then read aloud the definitions.

q u e s t i o n

question: a problem

q u i c k l y

quickly: very fast

q u i t e

quite: wholly

q u a d r i l a t e r a l

quadrilateral: four sides

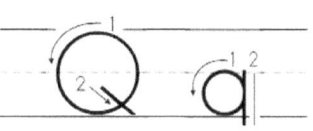 Use the examples
below to help write
new sentences.

I quickly solved a question.

She was **quite** surprised.

He drew a **quadrilateral**.

R r

Practice tracing the letters and then write them.

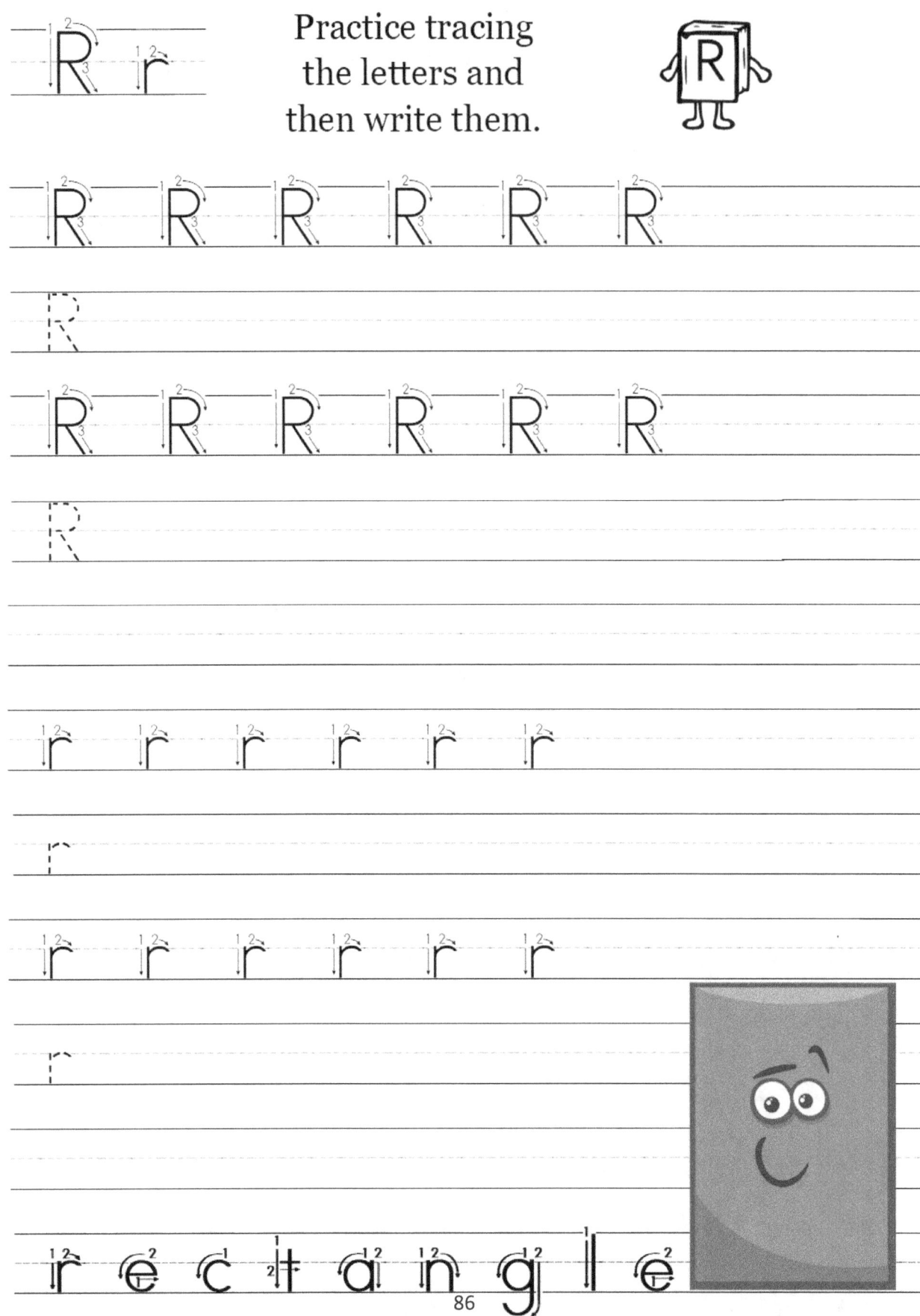

R R R R R R

R

R R R R R R

R

r r r r r r

r

r r r r r r

r

rectangle

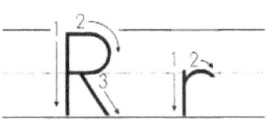

Trace and write
the sight words.

read
read

return
retun

right
right

rectangle
rectangle

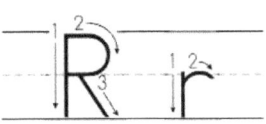 Trace and write the
sight words, then read
aloud the definitions.

read

read: to utter aloud

return

return: to go back

right

right: correct standard

rectangle

rectangle: Four right angles

Use the examples
below to help write
new sentences.

He **read** the **right** story.

She will **return** the book.

I saw the **rhombus** first.

BONUS WORDS FROM THE DANGER TWINS

The Danger Twins listed bonus sight words below. Write a sentence using any of the sight words.

quart   rake

quiz   ring

queen   round

S s

Practice tracing
the letters and
then write them.

S S S S S S

S

S S S S S S

S

S S S S S S

S

S S S S S S

S

s t a r

 **S s**

**Trace and write
the sight words.**

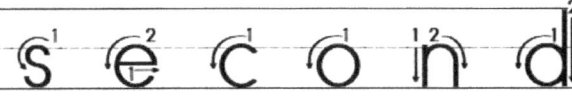 **s a w**

s a w

s e c o n d

s e c o n d

s t u d y

s t u d y

s t a r

s t a r

Trace and write the sight words, then read aloud the definitions.

s a w

saw: past tense of see

s e c o n d

second: after the first

s t u d y

study: to apply oneself

s t a r

star: five pointed shape

Use the examples
below to help write
new sentences.

She ate the **second** snack.

He **saw** the girl **study**.

We **saw** the **star**.

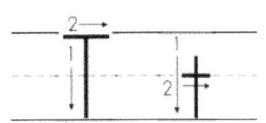

Practice tracing the letters and then write them.

T T T T T T

T

T T T T T T

T

t t t t t t

t

t t t t t t

t

triangle

96

T t

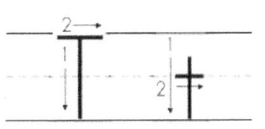

Trace and write the sight words.

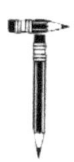

tiny

tiny

this

this

total

total

triangle

triangle

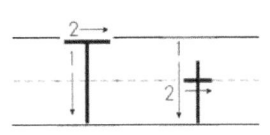

Trace and write the
sight words, then read
aloud the definitions.

tiny

tiny: not big

this

this: indicate a thing

total

total: whole; entire

triangle

triangle: three sides

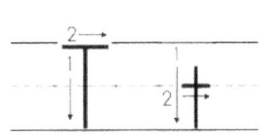 

Use the examples below to help write new sentences.

The sum **total** is missing.

She likes **this** workbook.

The **triangle** is tiny.

BONUS WORDS FROM THE DANGER TWINS

The Danger Twins listed bonus sight words below. Write a sentence using any of the sight words.

shark   tree

ship   teapot

seven   ten

U u

Practice tracing the letters and then write them.

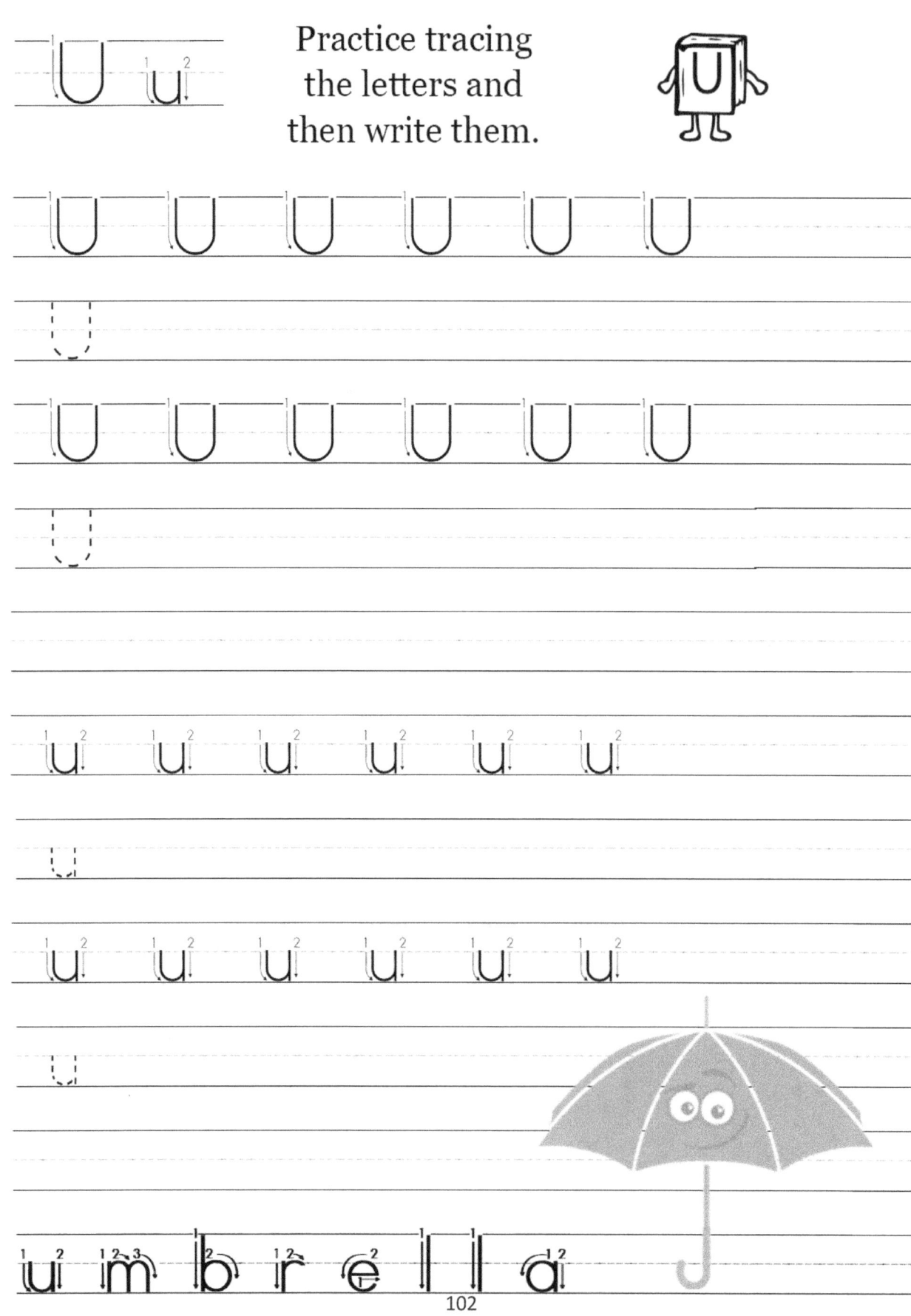

U U U U U U

U

U U U U U U

U

u u u u u u

u

u u u u u u

u

umbrella

102

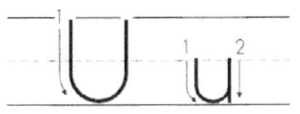

Trace and write
the sight words.

under

under

unit

unit

us

us

umbrella

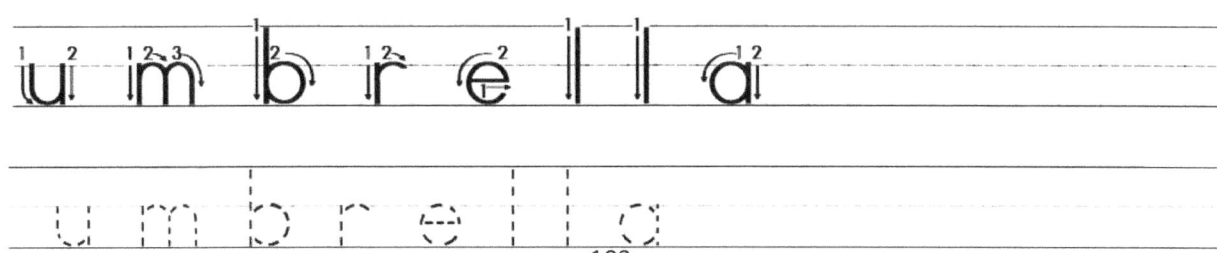

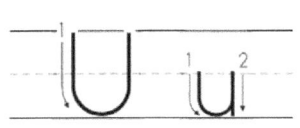 Trace and write the
sight words, then read
aloud the definitions.

under

under: beneath

unit

unit: a single thing; person

us

us: objective case of we

umbrella

umbrella: a cone shape

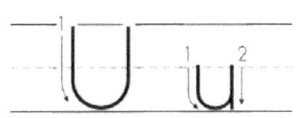

Use the examples
below to help write
new sentences.

One unit is full.

The cat is under us.

I opened the umbrella.

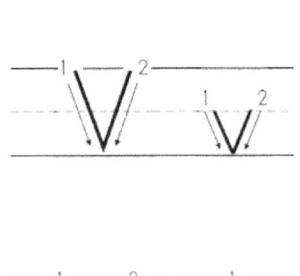

Practice tracing the letters and then write them.

V V V V V V V

V

V V V V V V

V

v v v v v v

v

v v v v v v

v

v a l e n t i n e

106

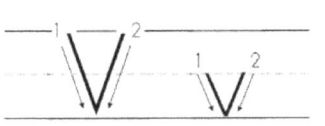

Trace and write the sight words.

value

value

voice

voice

vowel

vowel

valentine

valentine

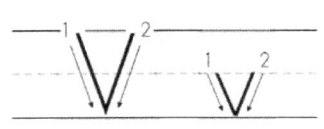 Trace and write the
sight words, then read
aloud the definitions.

value

value: of importance; merit

voice

voice: sound of speech

vowel

vowel: a, e, i, o, or u

valentine

valentine: heart shaped note

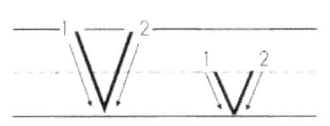 Use the examples
below to help write
new sentences.

Your **voice** has **value**.

He can say each **vowel**.

I drew the **valentine**.

BONUS WORDS FROM THE DANGER TWINS

The Danger Twins listed bonus sight words below. Write a sentence using any of the sight words.

until   vest

use   vase

up   view

W w

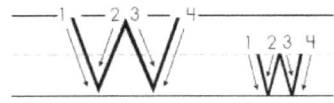

Practice tracing the letters and then write them.

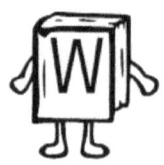

W W W W W

W

W W W W W

W

w w w w w w

w

w w w w w w

w

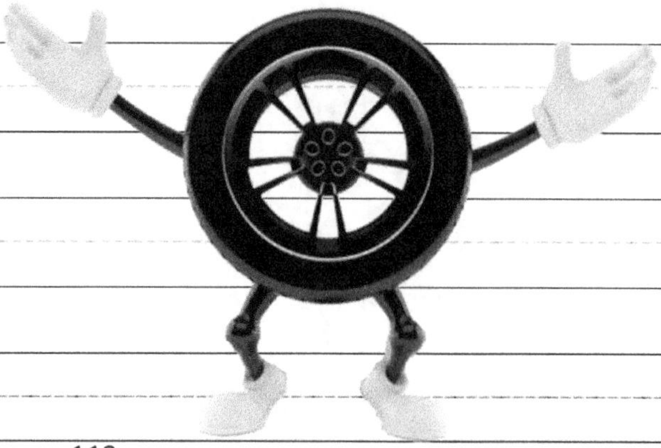

w h e e l

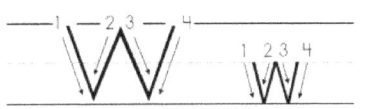 **Trace and write the sight words.**

way

way

well

well

wrong

wrong

wheel

wheel

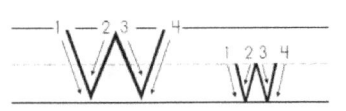 Trace and write the
sight words, then read
aloud the definitions.

w a y

way: manner; mode

w e l l

well: in a good manner

w r o n g

wrong: deviating from truth

w h e e l

wheel: has a circular shape

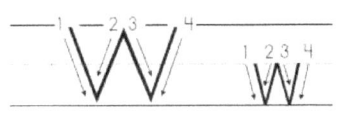 

Use the examples below to help write new sentences.

He went that **way**.

She is **well** mannered.

The **wheel** size is **wrong**.

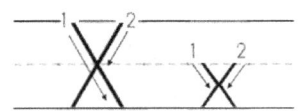

Practice tracing the letters and then write them.

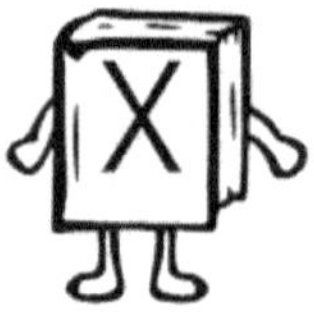

X X X X X X

X

X X X X X X

X

X X X X X X

X

X X X X X X

X

x-m a r k

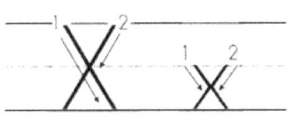

x y l o p h o n e

x e n o p s

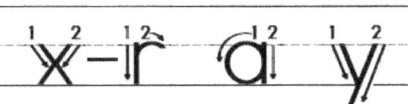

x-r a y

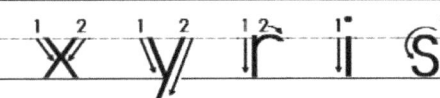

x y r i s

x y r i s

x-m a r k

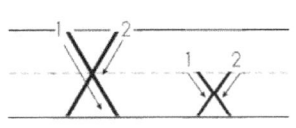

Trace and write the sight words, then read aloud the definitions.

x e n o p s

xenops: a type of bird

x-r a y

x-ray: a medical test

x y r i s

xyris: a type of flower

x-m a r k

x-mark: the exact location

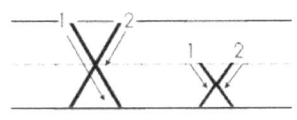

Use the examples
below to help write
new sentences.

A xenops flew to the xyris.

The x-ray was helpful.

The map has an x-mark.

BONUS WORDS FROM THE DANGER TWINS

The Danger Twins listed bonus sight words below. Write a sentence using any of the sight words.

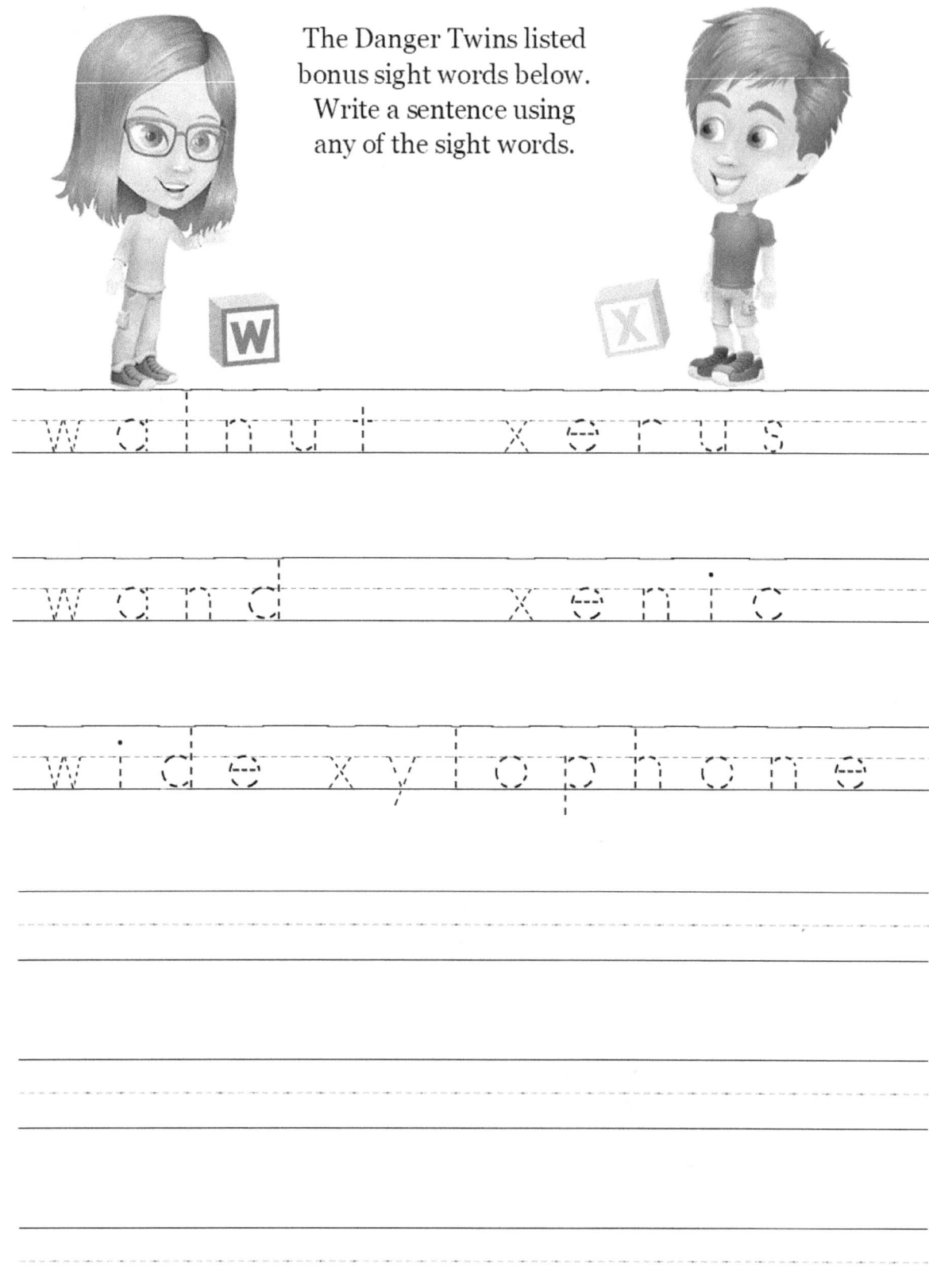

walnut xerus

wand xenic

wide xylophone

Y y

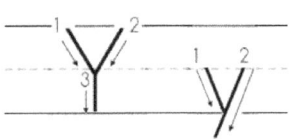

Practice tracing the letters and then write them.

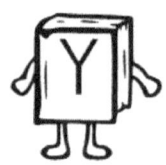

Y Y Y Y Y Y

Y

Y Y Y Y Y Y

Y

y y y y y y

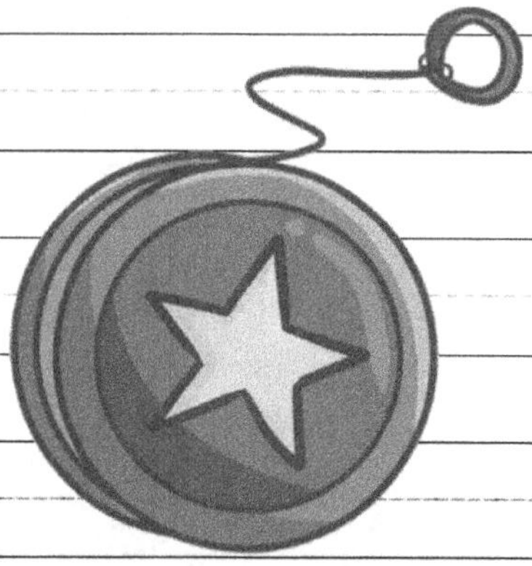

y

y y y y y y

y

yo-yo

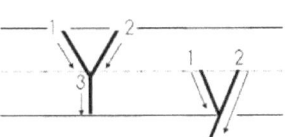

Trace and write
the sight words.

years

years

yes

yes

young

young

yo-yo

yo-yo

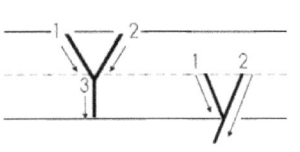 

Trace and write the sight words, then read aloud the definitions.

years

years: 12 months each year

yes

yes: an affirmative reply

young

young: not old

yo-yo

yo-yo: a string toy

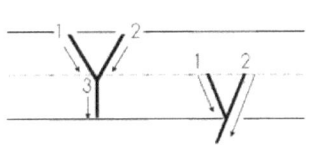

Use the examples
below to help write
new sentences.

I lived there five years.

That is a young puppy.

Yes, I like the yo-yo.

Z z

Practice tracing
the letters and
then write them.

Z Z Z Z Z Z

Z

Z Z Z Z Z Z

Z

z z z z z z

z

z z z z z z

z

zig zag

126

Zz

Trace and write the sight words.

zest

zest

zipping

zipping

zoo

zoo

zigzag

zigzag

Zz

Trace and write the
sight words, then read
aloud the definitions.

z e s t

zest: hearty enjoyment

z i p p i n g

zipping: move with speed

z o o

zoo: animals are kept here

z i g z a g

zigzag: up and down shape

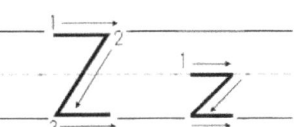

Use the examples
below to help write
new sentences.

They were **zipping** with **zest.**

The boy was at the **zoo.**

I ran in a **zigzag** pattern.

BONUS WORDS FROM THE DANGER TWINS

The Danger Twins listed bonus sight words below. Write a sentence using any of the sight words.

yours   zebra

your   zipper

years   zero

theDangerTwins.com